YOU KNOW YOUR CAT LOVES YOU BECAUSE...

The Sweet, Silly, and Scientific Ways Our Cats Show Us How Much They Love Us

by Jeff Parks and Nina Brissey
illustrations by Mark Sean Wilson

YOU KNOW YOUR CAT
LOVES YOU BECAUSE...

For permission requests, write to the publisher at:
youknowyourcatlovesyoubecause@gmail.com

Printed in the United States of America
ISBN: 978-0-692-07481-7
First Printing: 2019

Illustrations and Cover Art: Mark Sean Wilson
Editor: Cynthia Tews
Art Director: Nina Brissey

To our cats: Windows, Macready, and Sinbad.

Thank you for the inspiration. This book wouldn't exist without you. You three are loved more than you could ever know.

You Have a Special Connection with Your Cat

You know what every meow means, what every lift of the tail signals, what your cat likes, and of course, what they dislike. (Doorbells, they dislike doorbells.)

When I turn on the TV, my little Macky bounces out of the bedroom, hops on the recliner, and lays down next to me. When you open your heart to a cat, they return your devotion in unique ways...Or do they?

Some scientific studies claim that what we see as love from our cats is simply an evolutionary trait, not true emotional bonding. They argue that cats learned to show affection solely to get food and care. To that we say, "Baloney!" We know our cats love us as much as we love them. And we decided to prove it.

After combing through scientific data, countless stories from cat owners, and our own lifetime of experiences, the results are in: Far from being the distant or aloof animals depicted in popular media, cats are indeed capable of showing love in a multitude of ways. Ways you may never have known or imagined.

From the scientific, to the sweet, to the silly, this book illustrates all the ways our cats indisputably love us!

When you close your door, they meow, scratch, and bang to get in. Whatever they need to do to get to you, they will do it.

When you're sick, they stay close until you feel better.

They create beautiful art for you. They transform your plain, ordinary toilet paper into beautiful, exotic, origami art you can proudly display on your walls.

They brush up against you to mark their territory. Some animals mark their territory with pee, so consider yourself lucky.

They haven't destroyed your vacuum cleaner, even though it's their natural enemy.

They hate chasing lasers, but do it anyway because they know you love watching them. Though the truth is, they'd rather make you chase lasers that can't be caught.

When you're having a bad day, they groom you and make you smile.

They bring you gifts. Wonderful gifts, like dead rats, dead birds, and live fleas. All for you. All for love.

When they see you crying, they don't try to comfort you. They respect your independence and know you need your personal space during this emotional time.

They make sure there is always a part of them near you, as all your clothes have cat hair on them.

The slow, long blinks they give you are kitty code for "I love you."

Sometimes they walk across your back and give you a massage.

When you're on the phone they meow at you to hang up and spend time with them. Either that or they have an important call to make.

They don't try scaring you by jumping out from the dark, and yes, they are familiar with horror movies.

They throw up a lot, but never on your remote.

When you're on the toilet, they come and hang out with you. Now that's love. Love, and the ability to hold their breath for long stretches of time.

They keep an eye out for strangers lurking near your house.

They're always smacking stuff off tables just to get you to do some cardio for the day.

They wrap their tail around you to let you know that you are theirs, and you're not going anywhere.

They sit on your laptop, protecting it from theft…
and from you using it. But mostly
for the theft reason.

They haven't spilled any of your deepest, darkest secrets…and they know them all.

They play in every cardboard box you open since they know you find it cute. But, they do find it kind of humiliating when you post a photo of it on social media.

When you pet them a few times and walk away,
they meow at you to come back and
keep giving them love.

They do amazing, hard-to-learn tricks. Like the one where they pretend not to notice you after you repeatedly call their name from only two feet away.

You still have fingers after giving them oral medicine.

Sometimes they come to you when you call them Captain Meow Meow of the S.S. Kitty.

They show you their belly, which is their most vulnerable spot.

They show you why buying new furniture
would be a waste of money.

They pass gas, but you never hear it,
and more importantly, never smell it.

When you're sleeping and can't keep an eye on them, they wake you up at 4am to let you know they're ok. It's also ok to feed them now, as long as you're up and all.

Sometimes when you stare at them, their pupils expand and they show you the universe in their eyes.

They give you love taps with their head, also known as "bunting."

They never pee on your bed. Never, unless of course you take them to the vet, then yeah, your cat is definitely peeing on your bed.

They constantly get in your way just to be near you, even if it means they get bumped around a bit.

They never try to eat your food, even when it's left in plain sight.

Your favorite sweater is also their favorite.

They aren't afraid to tell you when you've had too much to drink.

They enjoy playing with you, but don't need you doting on them 24/7.

They watch TV with you even though you never watch what they want to watch.

They groom their face every day in order to look their best for you.

When they're sleeping and you kiss them on the head, they don't jump and instinctively slash your face with their claws.

When you put a Santa hat on them for a Christmas picture, they let you take the photo. Though in truth, they find it beneath their dignity.

They still go to sleep with you at night, even though they're nocturnal creatures.

If they mistakenly do their business outside their litter box, they try to cover it with imaginary litter to spare your sense of smell…and well being.

They never use their claws when they settle snugly into your lap.

They are nowhere to be found when you enter the house. They know you need your decompression time after work…at least until it's time to feed them.

Sometimes you wake up and they're right next to you.

You gave them a bath that one time and lived to tell about it.

They don't get jealous or mad when they see you watching cat videos on the internet.

You Know Your Cat Loves You Because…

They get more affectionate
as they get older.

Nina Brissey does a little bit of everything. Acting, writing, directing, producing, sewing, remodeling, and hanging out with family, friends, and, of course, animals. She is a dog-mommy to her rescue German Shepherd, Bruce. Nina grew up with a Rottweiler, Lancer, and a black cat, Sinbad. All the treats in the world would never be enough to repay her K-9 and feline friends for the love they've given her.

Jeff Parks is a freelance writer and editor. He shares a home in Temecula, California, with his spirited and wonderful cat, Mac.

Mark Sean Wilson has been scratching his way to the top of the illustrator heap his whole life. He is fascinated with illustration and cartoons but he didn't truly go professional with his talents until he earned an associate degree in graphic design and multimedia. He has since been illustrating children's books and comics for 25 years. You can see Mark's work at www.markerdoodle.com.

Made in the USA
Middletown, DE
18 April 2020